THE POWER OF
FAITH
A DAILY GUIDE TO VICTORY

Now Faith Is The Substance Of Things Hoped For,
The Evidence Of Things Not Seen.
Hebrews 11:1 KJV

The Overcomer

THE POWER OF FAITH

A DAILY GUIDE TO VICTORY

Now Faith Is The Substance Of Things Hoped For,
The Evidence Of Things Not Seen.
Hebrews 11:1 KJV

The Overcomer

TESTIMONY

It was a disaster day on my way to my second job, I was involved in a hit and run accident on my motorcycle. I only had 3 choices, to either go left into oncoming traffic and hit a truck, or go right and hit the back of the car and have another car quickly coming up in that lane to hit me as well, or keep moving forward and trust God to bring me through this situation. I made a choice to trust God and His wisdom though it did not make sense to me at the moment. Many things that we deal with from day to day may not make sense at the time though we move forward trusting in the direction that has been given. Once I landed on the ground I was in terrible pain, looking upward and all I could find myself to do was thank God and ask that He put my family at peace as the young lady that stopped to assist me informed me that someone named Thomas was calling. Thomas is our youngest son and he was informed that I had come to an abrupt stop and was trying to reach me. Even though we experience trials and tribulations we are to thank God in the midst of our situation to acknowledge Him and His will for our lives. Within 2 minutes an unmarked police car arrived as well and shortly afterward the Memphis Fire Department was on the scene. All I cared about was that my family was not worried about me and I wanted to reach out to them, though the EMT had to do their job to assist me and I had to submit to their request. Once in the back of the vehicle an officer began asking for my information and was informed that I could give it to them despite how I may have appeared. As I was giving my name the officer stated that the name sounded familiar after looking at my driver's license, he said Bernard this is Brandon your cousin and an answer to my prayers. I asked him to reach out to my wife to assure her that I was alright. Once the EMT had completed starting an ivy and administered pain medication, I asked for my phone to contact my family via text because my phone was malfunctioning and also reached out to my employer via text. The ride was slow and rough though the EMTs were a God send as they tended to my injuries. They finally removed my helmet and placed a collar on my neck for stability. Today I am alive with my family through Faith in God, all glory be to Jesus our Comforter.

Have Faith In God!
The Overcomer

Table Of Content

TESTIMONY
INTRODUCTION

DAY ELEVEN
TOPIC: GOD IS ALIVE

DAY TWELVE
TOPIC: TAKE RESPONSIBILITY FOR YOUR FAITH GROWTH

DAY THIRTEEN
TOPIC: ALIVE BY FAITH

DAY FOURTEEN
TOPIC: WORKING BY THE SPIRIT

DAY FIFTEEN
TOPIC: FOCUS ON GOD

DAY SIXTEEN
TOPIC: TRUST IN THE LORD

DAY SEVENTEEN
TOPIC: SEEK THE GUIDANCE OF GOD

DAY EIGHTEEN
TOPIC: BUILD A SOLID RELATIONSHIP WITH GOD

DAY NINETEEN
TOPIC: SPEND TIME WITH HIM THROUGH PRAYER AND BY READING HIS WORD

DAY TWENTY
TOPIC: TALK TO GOD EVERYWHERE

DAY TWENTY ONE
TOPIC: LISTEN TO GOD'S VOICE AND PRACTICE OBEDIENCE TO HIS WORD

DAY TWENTY TWO

TOPIC: INVITE HIM TO COME CLOSE

DAY TWENTY THREE
TOPIC: TAKE THE TIME TO TOUCH BASES WITH GOD

DAY TWENTY FOUR
TOPIC: OBEY GOD'S COMMANDMENTS.

DAY TWENTY FIVE
TOPIC: CONTINUE WORKING ON YOUR SALVATION.

DAY TWENTY SIX
TOPIC: DON'T COMPARE YOUR RELATIONSHIP WITH GOD TO THAT OF OTHERS

DAY TWENTY SEVEN
TOPIC: PLACE YOUR REQUEST BEFORE GOD

DAY TWENTY EIGHT
TOPIC: SEEK HELP FROM GOD

DAY TWENTY NINE
TOPIC: YOU CAN DO ALL THINGS THROUGH HIM

DAY THIRTY
TOPIC: YOU WILL OVERCOME

Conclusion

INTRODUCTION

Now faith is the substance of things hoped for, the evidence of things not seen...Hebrews 11:1

"Now faith means that we are confident of what we hope for, convinced of what we do not see."

"Faith gives substance to our hopes." Another translation says, "Faith is the warranty deed that the thing for which you have fondly hoped is at last yours.

The Spirit, through Paul, is simply telling us that faith is laying hold of the unrealities of hope and bringing them into the realm of reality.

You hope for finances to meet the obligations you have, but faith gives you the assurance you'll have the money when you need it. You hope for physical strength to do the job you must do, but faith says, "The Lord is the strength of my life; of whom shall I be afraid?" (Ps. 27:1).

Faith, we know, grows out of the Word of God: "So then faith cometh by hearing, and hearing by the word of God" (Rom. 10:17).

Here is a little formula of faith patterned after Abraham's faith which you can make work for you:

First, Abraham had God's Word for it.

Second, Abraham believed God's Word.

Third, Abraham considered not the contradictory circumstances.

Fourth, Abraham gave praise to God.

Follow those four steps and you'll always get through to God. They are four steps to certain deliverance, healing, or whatever you are seeking. This is What you are about to learn through daily communication with God and prayer to increase you in Christ Jesus our Lord. Amen

DAY ONE

TOPIC: FAITH

Bible Reading: Hebrews 11:1

1. "Now faith is the substance of things hoped for, the evidence of things not seen".

Memory Verse: Hebrews 11:6

> *"But without faith it is impossible to please Him, for he who comes to God must believe that He is, and that He is a rewarder of those who diligently seek Him".*

Massage

Faith's eye sees beyond our current circumstances and roots itself in divine revelation revealed by almighty God through the Word-made-flesh. We believes that Scripture contain God's truth, which was written for our learning, education, encouragement, (2 Timothy 3:16) and hope. Even when life's circumstances appear to contradict the truth of God's Word, the heart of faith allows us to treat the unseen as real.

Sometime ago, I had an accident on my way going to work, it was hit and run accident on my motorcycle. It was a terrible incident which took three different dimension my motorcycle goes left into oncoming traffic and hit a truck, then turn right and hit the back of the car and have another car quickly coming up in that lane to hit me as well. The condition seen never to be recovery to be change anymore, but I keep moving forward and trust God to bring me through the situation. I made a choice to trust and believe God and His wisdom, though it did not make sense to me at the moment. My faith in God yielded a timely result and there was help for me, out of that ugly situation.

Many things that we deal with from day to day may not make sense at the time though we move forward trusting and having faith in the direction that has been given by God.

Faith is not based on experience, nor calculated through reason. True faith is anchored on scriptural facts. It is beyond man's intellect and cannot be penetrated through reasoning or discovered through scientific 'proof'. It has nothing to do with personal opinion or impressions. It is beyond the dimension of human thought because it is the substance of facts that are conceived in the mind of God. Is there any condition or circumstance that seems impossible to change or go through? The bible says, there's nothing too hard of impossible to do, just have faith in Him and He will down around circumstance for good.

PRAYER POINT: *Loving Father, I can be so entrenched in my own thinking that sometimes I doubt Your Word and question Your promises, please help my unbelief, Thank You for the gift of faith, and I pray that day by day my loving trust in You and the reality of Your Word will become increasingly established within my heart in Jesus' name I pray, AMEN.*

DAY TWO

TOPIC: PURPOSE OF FAITH

Bible Reading: Ephesians 2:8–10

8. For by grace you have been saved through faith, and that not of yourselves; it is the gift of God
9. Not of works, lest anyone should boast.
10. For we are His workmanship, created in Christ Jesus for good works, which God prepared beforehand that we should walk in them.

Memory Verse: James 2:26

"26 For as the body without the spirit is dead, so faith without works is dead also.".

Massage

Without faith, we couldn't expect that things would turn out all right for us no matter what the situation might be. Faith, then, is just as important as the air we breathe. While the oxygen in the air nourishes the body, faith nourishes the heart and the soul. It's the energy that courses through every single fiber and cell within our beings. It's part of every muscle and every strand of thought. It is the fundamental foundation of our existence.

People have moved mountains with their faith. Even when situations seemed dire and bleak, it was their faith that carried them through. There's little to no explanation for it in the physical realm; it's the metaphysical fiber that binds us all, carrying each of our deepest wishes and desires. That's where faith lives.

Unfortunately, some people don't believe in things that they cannot see. They explain things away due to other causes and effects, failing to find the small miracles in life that exist and work in our favour on a constant basis. There's an enormous level of importance attributable to having faith in life. Faith is the pathway for abundance, so be sure to hold it at the forefront of your mind. Don't be afraid to expect the very best for yourself. This isn't about being selfish or aimlessly wishing for things; this is about the true, utterance, deep-down belief in your heart and your soul that things will improve, and that you deserve the very best in life.

PRAYER POINT: *Loving Father, please grant me the grace to have faith in your word and grant me the grace to take the actions of faith in Jesus' name I pray, AMEN.*

DAY THREE

TOPIC: SUBMIT TO HIS WILL THROUGH FAITH

Bible Reading: Matthew 26:42

"He went away again a second time and prayed, saying, "My Father, if this cannot pass away unless I drink it, Your will be done."

Memory Verse: Psalms 143:10
"Teach me to do your will, for you are my God; let your good Spirit lead me on level ground."

Massage

We have once experienced a hard time in our lives and many times we felt during those days that it would never end and wondered if we would make it through the situation. In the midst of dark and troublesome circumstances God is reshaping and refining our characters to prepare us for the journey ahead. Just because we experience something that makes us uncomfortable and we do not understand, shift gears to operate in faith as we trust God to do whatever He deems necessary for our success in His will going forward.

Submitting to the will of God means dying to self, and living unto Him. It was the hallmark of the Apostle Paul and his ministry in submitting to God's will. There is a very clear structured design and direction for the ministry of one who is moving in the will of God. It is one thing to know the will of God and another is to act in line with the known will. The ultimate will of the father is to glorify His Holy name (1Cor 10:31). This is the primary essence of our faith on earth. Gods will for your life is not a separate plan from His will for His Kingdom.

PRAYER POINT: *Father we know that we are blessed and are not alone help us to always lean on You in Jesus name we pray amen, AMEN.*

DAY FOUR

TOPIC: YOUR FAITH DRAWS YOU NEAR TO GOD

Bible Reading: Hebrews 10:19-22

19 "Therefore, brethren, having boldness to enter the Holiest by the blood of Jesus,

20 by a new and living way which He consecrated for us, through the veil, that is, His flesh

21 and having a High Priest over the house of God

22 let us draw near with a true heart in full assurance of faith, having our hearts sprinkled from an evil conscience and our bodies washed with pure water".

Memory Verse: 1 Peter 3:18

"For Christ also died for sins once for all, the just for the unjust, in order that He might bring us to God."

Massage

Good morning, we have experienced many occasions where we did something that normally we would not have done and then we wonder to ourselves, what was I thinking? The more and more we spend time with our Father, the more He works through us when we would have otherwise responded in a different manner. Actually it is a perfect example of our surrendering to the will of God as the only mean of our survival. To surrender or submit to God and His Will on whatever thing or decision is not a sign of personal weakness but an act of our commitment to God regardless of our emotions.

Surrendering to God grants us the access to approach His throne of grace with confidence, so that we may receive mercy and find grace to help in time of our need (Heb. 4:16). That we come to him confident that he will reward us with all that he is for us in Jesus. And this is clearly what he means here in Hebrews 10:22, because verse 19 says that we have confidence "to enter the holy place," that is, the new heavenly "holy of holies" like that inner room in the old tabernacle of the Old Testament where the high priest met with God once a year, and where his glory descended on the ark of the covenant. As we continue our Christian race, let us build on our most holy faith, believing in His word of lives as the scripture says that let him that come to God believe that He is and is the rewarder of those that diligently seek Him (Heb. 11:6).

PRAYER POINT: *Draw us closer to you as we seek to be within your will, in Jesus name we pray, AMEN.*

DAY FIVE

TOPIC: WHEN YOU PRAY, YOU MUST BELIEVE

Bible Reading: James 1:6, 7

> 6. "But let him ask in faith, with no doubting, for he who doubts is like a wave of the sea driven and tossed by the wind.
> 7. For let not that man suppose that he will receive anything from the Lord".

Memory Verse: Mark 11:24

"Therefore, I say unto you, whatsoever things you desire, when you pray, believe that you receive them, and you shall have them".

Massage

There are many things that will happen in life that will cause us to question whether or not God is listening to our prayers, until we experience something that removes all doubt even if it appears tragic. God will use what appears apparently horrible at first sight to reveal His grace and mercy to those that may be questioning His ability to see His hand in a situation, as the scripture says that God hath chosen the foolish things of the world to confound the wise, and God hath chosen the weak things of the world to confound the things which are mighty (1 Corinthians 1:27). We that have chosen to follow God may be used as God sees fit to further His work and it may not necessarily be comfortable to us during the journey. Nevertheless, God will never send us anywhere that we will be without His presence.

The Bible tells us that we are not just to pray, but rather to pray believing. If we are specifically told to believe when we pray, then it must be possible to pray and not believe. Not all prayer brings results. Only believing prayer moves God and receives from Him, He says in His word that did I not say to you that if you would believe you would see the glory of God? (John 11:40). So as a Christian, you must learn to believe in His word in other to experience of His Glory.

PRAYER POINT: *Lord we are grateful for your wonderful wisdom in the midst of our mess in which you are preparing a masterpiece. You have equipped us for a time such as this to endure the storms that we may go through for your glory, in Jesus name we pray, AMEN.*

DAY SIX
TOPIC: THROUGH FAITH, WE WILL CONQUER

Bible Reading: Hebrews 11:33-35

33. who through faith subdued kingdoms, worked righteousness, obtained promises, stopped the mouths of lions,
34. quenched the violence of fire, escaped the edge of the sword, out of weakness were made strong, became valiant in battle, turned to flight the armies of the aliens. 35 Women received their dead raised to life again. Others were tortured, not accepting deliverance, that they might obtain a better resurrection".

Memory Verse: Romans 10:17
"So then faith comes by hearing, and hearing by the word of God".

Massage

Good morning, when we are going through difficult times we tend to become reluctant to do our personal best, though we do try to convince ourselves that we are. Be advised, that through it all we are to depend upon God to give us whatever we are in need of, endeavor to make it through every situation regardless of the severity of it. Our lives are not going to be continuously filled with all of our favorite things that we want to make us happy though it will be filled with the love of God and a peace that passes all understanding, filling our hearts with joy.

The scripture clearly states to us patriarchs who have endured and conquered. These people of faith "subdued kingdoms." The word translated "subdued" literally means "to conquer" or "to overcome." The root, speaks of engaging in a struggle or fight. This is precisely what they faced, and yet the Lord brought down the kingdoms because He was establishing His kingdom. We should take heart that He is still extending His kingdom and no earthly kingdom is a match for Him. We should expect such great things and then, like Gideon of old, went forth in faith, expecting the nations to bow the knee to our Lord and Saviour, Jesus Christ.

Jesus said in the Holy scripture that in the world, we will see tribulations, we only have to be of good cheer as He has overcame the world for us (John 16:33). Therefore, whatever circumstance that comes our way, we are to be with good cheer because God has already overcome it for us.

PRAYER POINT: *Lord we thank you for your continuous love and guidance in the midst of our lives on our journeys that have you as the common thread. May you continue to speak with us regarding your will for our lives and equip us as only you can for our journeys ahead in Jesus name we pray, AMEN.*

DAY SEVEN

TOPIC: FAITH BRINGS OPPORTUNITY TO US

Bible Reading: 1 Peter 1:6-7

6. "In this you greatly rejoice, though now for a little while, if need be, you have been grieved by various trials

7. that the genuineness of your faith, being much more precious than gold that perishes, though it is tested by fire, may be found to praise, honor, and glory at the revelation of Jesus Christ".

Memory Verse: Matthew 19:26

"But Jesus looked at them and said to them, "With men this is impossible, but with God all things are possible".

Massage

Good morning, we are blessed to have an opportunity to see another thankful day by way of God's grace and mercy towards us. Even though we experience rough times that may even rock the world as we know it, that does not prevent God from being there through it all. This is because the loving kindness of God and is His peace is not removed due to our circumstances or situations because He knows the expected end that He desires for us.

Peter says that our faith is like gold, as it is tested, it will begin to bring the impurities to the surface. When the impurities are removed our faith becomes more valuable. Gold is the standard by which we define value. We say things like, "worth its weight in gold", "the golden boy", and "the golden age". Our jewelry is made of gold and we trade with it. In Peter's world and in ours, gold was considered one of the most valuable things a person could have.

While gold is valuable, it is secondary to our faith. Gold can perish, but our faith will endure. A faith in Jesus Christ will carry us through this life and even into the world to come. A faith in the death, burial, and resurrection of God's only Son is far more valuable than gold. Our faith is in something eternal, not in something that can be destroyed.

PRAYER POINT: *Father we are thankful that you are not like man that can be shaken by changes in our lives and faithful towards us always, in Jesus name we pray, AMEN.*

DAY EIGHT
TOPIC: BELIEVE AND TRUST THE PROCESS
Bible Reading: Isaiah 40:31

31 But those who wait on the Lord Shall renew their strength; they shall mount up with wings like eagles, they shall run and not be weary, they shall walk and not faint.

Memory Verse: 2 Corinthians 5:7
7 *"For we walk by faith, not by sight".*
Massage

Good morning, we have experienced a hard time or two in our lives and many times we felt during those days that it would never end and wondered if we would make it through the situation. In the midst of dark and troublesome circumstances God is reshaping and refining our characters to prepare us for the journey ahead. Just because we experience something that makes us uncomfortable and we do not understand, shift gears to operate in faith as we trust God to do whatever He deems necessary for our success in His will going forward.

How can you learn to trust the process? In other words, how can you trust life, and that everything will be ok? First, we must learn to develop trust and the optimal way to trust is to trust things that are trustworthy. I know it is hard to trust people at times especially if you have had your heart broken. When people lose trust, they lose trust in people. I will say this, there is nothing more trustworthy than God. He is truthful and worthy! If you begin to trust someone who is trustworthy then you will see that the process is worth it. Then you can trust people who look to Him, reflect His very character, and love.

PRAYER POINT: *Father we know that we are blessed and are not alone help us to always lean on you in Jesus name we pray, AMEN.*

DAY NINE

TOPIC: FORGET YOUR WORRIES, GOD IS AT WORK IN YOU

Bible Reading: Matthew 11:28-30

28 "Come to Me, all you who labor and are heavy laden, and I will give you rest.
29 Take My yoke upon you and learn from Me, for I am gentle and lowly in heart, and you will find rest for your souls.
30 For My yoke is easy and my burden is light."

Memory Verse: Philippians 4:6
6 "Be anxious for nothing, but in everything by prayer and supplication, with thanksgiving, let your requests be made known to God".

Massage

Good morning, we may have had experiences that we had questions about our well being due to an unfortunate situation. Though we are instructed to worry not because God knows and is well aware of what we are in need of. What we are to do is seek after God and His Kingdom and all else will be added unto us. We should learn not to our own understanding concerning the events that occur in our lives.

I've been guilty on more than one occasion of praying and leaving my quiet time with more anxiety than when I started. How can this be? If I give my worries to God, shouldn't I be feeling much lighter? He created us and all our emotions. And remember, he called his creation good!
Jesus himself was tempted by everything we face and certainly displayed anger, anguish, sadness, and grief. Each of these feelings can, however, easily lead worry (Heb.4:15).

God wants a clear path to our heart at all times. As we learn to accept rather than suppress our emotions, we can start the practice of being honest with God. He wants every good thing for us and a close relationship with him is the very best starting point.

PRAYER POINT: *Lord, please help us not to worry because you are faithful in all of your ways concerning our lives and our needs, in Jesus name we pray, AMEN.*

DAY TEN
TOPIC: BUILD YOUR FAITH DAILY
Bible Reading: Romans 10:17; Joshua 1:8

Romans 10:17
17. So then faith comes by hearing, and hearing by the word of God".

Joshua 1:8
8 This Book of the Law shall not depart from your mouth, but you shall meditate in it day and night, that you may observe to do according to all that is written in it. For then you will make your way prosperous, and then you will have good success".

Memory Verse: Ephesians 2:8
8 "For by grace you have been saved through faith, and that not of yourselves; it is the gift of God".

Massage

Trials and tribulations will come and that should not be a surprise since we have been forewarned by God of this fact. Though when we are in the midst of such times we seem to forget that fact as well as the fact that we are not alone, for God also stated that He would never leave us nor forsake us. Just because we are not seeing God react as we expect we should not lose all hope, for this is a time we should work on our patience muscles as well as our faith in our father. Just like routines in our daily lives help us grow, establishing faith routines can help us grow in our relationship with God and build our faith.

Faith comes by hearing and hearing the word of God. To build your faith in God you need to consistently hear the word of God. You need to fill your life with the word not just on Sundays but everyday. Listen to the messages of your pastor and other faith preachers. The more you hear God's word the more your faith will grow as it will cause you to stay focused on the word. Think on the word of God and keep confessing it. As you do so you'll receive insight into the word of God.

PRAYER POINT: *Help us to grow in our ways concerning you Lord, in Jesus name we pray, AMEN.*

DAY ELEVEN
TOPIC: GOD IS ALIVE

Bible Reading: Revelation 1:4-6

Revelation 1:4-6

4. John, to the seven churches which are in Asia: Grace to you and peace from Him who is and who was and who is to come, and from the seven Spirits who are before His throne.
5. and from Jesus Christ, the faithful witness, the firstborn from the dead, and the ruler over the kings of the earth, To Him who loved us and washed us from our sins in His own blood.
6. and has made us kings and priests to His God and Father, to Him be glory and dominion forever and ever. Amen"

Memory Verse: ***Hebrews 4:12***

"For the word of God is living and powerful, and sharper than any two-edged sword, piercing even to the division of soul and spirit, and of joints and marrow, and is a discerner of the thoughts and intents of the heart."

Massage

The God of the Bible, the God we adore, is alive and healthy, according to today's verses. "Who was, who is, and who will be," he says. These comments serve as a reminder to everyone that the universe is also under the control of this eternal God. He is the "ruler of the kings of the earth." His Son, the Lord Jesus Christ, has come to us as "the trustworthy witness, the firstborn from the dead."

I know that there is a God; I absolutely and positively believe that God is real. With that being said one would believe that my faith is as strong and solid as it could be. As I was believing God to turn a situation around, I clearly owned as though I created the situation, I found myself questioning if my prayers were reaching God, whether or not He could hear my prayers, even if my faith was strong enough to warrant a response. Therefore, whatever situation that comes your way, tell it to the father and believe that it is already settled.

PRAYER POINT: ***Lord, please use us to spread the word that you are forever alive. And, Lord Jesus, we beg you to come speedily, AMEN.***

DAY TWELVE

TOPIC: TAKE RESPONSIBILITY FOR YOUR FAITH GROWTH

Bible Reading: 1 Corinthians 1:10

10 "Now I plead with you, brethren, by the name of our Lord Jesus Christ, that you all speak the same thing, and that there be no divisions among you, but that you be perfectly joined together in the same mind and in the same judgment".

Memory Verse: 2 Peter 1:10

10 "Therefore, brethren, be even more diligent to make your call and election sure, for if you do these things you will never stumble"

Massage

It is far more important to acquire self-discipline and live a Christian life in the Christian race, where everyone who crosses the finish line – not just the first – has an opportunity to earn the incorruptible crown, which is the eternal wealth of heaven. We have a habit of always blaming the devil for whatever unfortunate situation that happens in our lives and the truth of the matter is that why would the devil even bother with us when we are doing such a good job. See, the devil is very limited, he is not like God no matter how much he wants to be, though the greater threat is ourselves. We are our own worst enemy and once we get ourselves in check then we might be an adversary of the devil.

Knowledge is power regardless of what it is concerning as it causes growth and we are responsible for the direction in which we have chosen to go. I want to provide this disclaimer, I am not nor have I ever been perfect and we are going to rehash and dissect my life experiences in Hope's that we can better grow forward where our prayer life and faith is concerned on the remaining time of our lives journeys. You need to be intentional about your growth system as pertaining to your faith in Christ.

PRAYER POINT: *"Lord please grant me the grace to pay the price to receive my crown in Heaven, in Jesus name," AMEN.*

DAY THIRTEEN
TOPIC: ALIVE BY FAITH

Bible Reading: Ephesians 2:8-9

8. For by grace you have been saved through faith, and that not of yourselves; it is the gift of God
9. not of works, lest anyone should boast".

Memory Verse: Ephesians 1:14
14 "who is the guarantee of our inheritance until the redemption of the purchased possession, to the praise of His glory".

Massage

We would be able to brag when we attained the required level of righteousness to merit redemption if the plan and method of salvation were devised by ourselves, based on our good works. "I succeeded!" or "I gave it my all and overcame great obstacles, but in the end, I flew to the highest peaks of virtue and purity, and God gave me exactly what I deserved!" We could say of those who didn't make it, "Those others failed because they lacked the guts, wisdom, and piety that I cultivated."

There would be a considerable measure of confidence. If the aim and manner of redemption were based on human labor, we would elevate ourselves above other people and even God Himself, because our salvation was our own doing, not His. The plan and method of salvation are a gift from God, they are grace-based, and are accessed via faith in God's promises in Christ. Salvation is not something we achieve through our own efforts, nor is it based on our good deeds. Let the one who boasts boast in the Lord.

PRAYER POINT: ***"Lord please help give my faith life in Jesus name", AMEN.***

DAY FOURTEEN

TOPIC: WORKING BY THE SPIRIT

Bible Reading: Galatians 5:16-18

16. I say then: Walk in the Spirit, and you shall not fulfill the lust of the flesh.
17. For the flesh lusts against the Spirit, and the Spirit against the flesh; and these are contrary to one another, so that you do not do the things that you wish.
18. But if you are led by the Spirit, you are not under the law".

Memory Verse: Galatians 5:16
16 "I say then: Walk in the Spirit, and you shall not fulfill the lust of the flesh".

Massage

Walking by the spirit is the same as living a life in the spirit. It entails living your entire life in the presence of God's spirit. Jesus said in John 15 that we must abide in him, which is essentially the same thing. If we stay in Jesus, the spirit is at work within us. As we abide in Jesus Christ, as we abide in that vine, as a branch abides in the vine, the Holy Spirit is infusing sap into our bodies. And he is bearing fruit in our lives. "I shrivel up and die when I'm away from that vine," Jesus said.

As a result, walking in the spirit necessitates a sense of God. It's putting Christ first in your life over anything else. It's obeying God with your whole heart, as the Great Commandment demands. It entails having no other gods or idols before God and dedicating your life to Him.

When we talk about dwelling in Jesus, I believe it's also important to remember that one of the ways we do so is through spiritual disciplines. I won't be able to stay in Jesus by doing whatever I want. That is why the bible says that commit your ways into His Hands and He will direct thy paths (Prov. 3:6).

PRAYER POINT: *Lord, the grace to walk in the spirit be released upon me in Jesus name, AMEN.*

DAY FIFTEEN

TOPIC: FOCUS ON GOD

Bible Reading: 2 Corinthians 4:18

18 "while we do not look at the things which are seen, but at the things which are not seen. For the things which are seen are temporary, but the things which are not seen are eternal".

Memory Verse: John 10:29

29 'My Father, who has given them to Me, is greater than all; and no one is able to snatch them out of My Father's hand".

Massage

God's word is our guide, and we must be well-versed in it if we are to closely follow and focus on Him. After all, how can we concentrate on someone we don't know well? If you've been putting off Bible study because you're having trouble understanding God's word, don't let it stop you any longer. Honestly before my life had really begun I was wrecking it and really wanted to get my life back on track.

I began going to church with a female friend and at first it was for what was to come after service and later it was because of what was happening in the service. What changed? Plain and simple it was due to my desire for change in which I did not realize had everything to do with my relationship with God or rather the lack thereof.

Be advised that this very well may be a time in life where the oppose of God may frequent our door steps in order to redirect our focus. I was no different, the more focused I became on getting an understanding; I was being distracted during service in my attempt to discover what I needed to do. It does not matter what we are going through, our willingness to find truth will always lead to God for He is Truth.

PRAYER POINT: *Help us to focus on You in everyday of our lives, AMEN.*

DAY SIXTEEN

TOPIC: TRUST IN THE LORD

Bible Reading: Proverbs 3:5-6

5 "Trust in the Lord with all your heart, And lean not on your own understanding;

6 In all your ways acknowledge Him, And He shall direct your paths".

Memory Verse: Romans 8:28
28 "And we know that all things work together for good to those who love God, to those who are the called according to His purpose".

Massage

Let us walk through this minor miracle, this was after my sister graduated from high school and was supposed to be going on her senior trip. My mom had already said yes though when it came time for her to go she experienced a case of bills and was not in a position to provide her with the money needed. I immediately instructed my sister to pack her bags; she did not question me as to why or how she simply trusted that I was able to make it happen. During that time I was still at home and working as much as possible.

I had money in the bank and several uncashed paychecks on my dresser. The bank was closed and I did not have an ATM card, I was nervous that I would not be able to help my sister, so I went to the liquor store where I first began cashing my checks. As I began getting out of the car two very beautiful women stopped me and stated that the store was closed. Keep in mind that even though I noticed that the two women were beautiful and my normal response would have been to engage in conversation with them and see where we could go from there, my focus was on helping my sister and superseded my own wants, needs, and or desires at that time. I was about to get back in my car when I heard a knock on the glass door of the store and a young woman motioning for me to come back to the store.

The young woman let me in and cashed my check and I left my phone number with her to call me later that evening. She did not, though my sister was able to go on her first of many trips to come and I was happy to have been in a position to assist. Looking back at the situation God was trying to direct my attention to Him, by closing doors and placing me in a situation where I had to look for a miracle as He provided.

PRAYER POINT: *Oh God, please grant me the grace to trust in you always, in Jesus name AMEN.*

DAY SEVENTEEN

TOPIC: SEEK THE GUIDANCE OF GOD

Bible Reading: Proverbs 3:5-6

5 "Trust in the Lord with all your heart and lean not on your own understanding;

6 in all your ways submit to him, and he will make your paths straight".

Memory Verse: Isaiah 30:21

21 "Your ears shall hear a word behind you, saying, "This is the way, walk in it, "Whenever you turn to the right hand or whenever you turn to the left".

Massage

We can get so caught up in our perception of what is right and wrong by our evaluation of our situation that we forget that we are not to judge though we should certainly seek out the Lord for guidance and direction concerning every area of our lives.

This all occurred when I was relatively new in my relationship with God and I was afraid because nothing that I had ever been a part of was good enough nor successful and I believe that I had sabotaging our relationship.

It`s easy to take care of oneself though when another person is added into the equation it can become frustrating and we can make it even more difficult by trying to take things into our own hands. There may be a way that seems right to a man though it does not necessarily nor immediately make it right, it can definitely make a matter worse. It has been stated on more than one occasion that communication is the key in every relationship be it, family, friend, foe or even God.

PRAYER POINT: *Lord please help us to trust in you always that we should not gratify the will of the devil, in Jesus name we pray, AMEN.*

DAY EIGHTEEN
TOPIC: BUILD A SOLID RELATIONSHIP WITH GOD

Bible Reading: Deuteronomy 31:6

6 "Be strong and of good courage, do not fear nor be afraid of them; for the LORD your God, He is the One who goes with you. He will not leave you nor forsake you."

Memory Verse: John 14:6

Jesus said to him, "I am the way, the truth, and the life. No one comes to the Father except through Me.

Massage

I developed an individual relationship with God in the wake of encountering a few difficulties and challenges that I realized no one but He alone could assist me with surviving. While I knew a great deal about God essentially the entirety of my life, it required a long time to come to truly know him. It's never sufficient to simply be aware of God since when difficult situations come, you can't incline toward your insight into him for strength. You need to incline toward him. Frankly, you don't have to encounter a predicament to start fostering an individual relationship with God, you can begin at this moment.

In this way, on the off chance that you're in any way similar to me, and you know everyone of the things about church and Christianity, yet you feel that your relationship with God is not right, I need to direct you through the means I took as I developed nearer to God. I likewise believe you should realize that an individual relationship with God is certainly not something distant that main your minister or profound pioneer can accomplish. God wants to know everyone of his children personally, and that includes you.

PRAYER POINT: *Help us to grow in our ways concerning you Lord, in Jesus name we pray, AMEN.*

DAY NINETEEN

TOPIC: SPEND TIME WITH HIM THROUGH PRAYER AND BY READING HIS WORD

Bible Reading: James 4:8

8 "Draw near to God and He will draw near to you. Cleanse your hands, you sinners; and purify your hearts, you double-minded".

Memory Verse: Isaiah 1:18

18 "Come now, and let us reason together," Says the Lord, "Though your sins are like scarlet, They shall be as white as snow; Though they are red like crimson, They shall be as wool.

Massage

it is exceptionally evident that perhaps the main thing about being a Christian and building our relationship with Jesus Christ is creating time for God. Yet, all things considered, we need to focus on Jesus and remember Him for our everyday timetable, in the way that we can. (Regardless of whether you need to stick an update on your washroom reflect!) The Bible isn't only there to recount to you the narrative of Jesus Christ. The narratives that are important for the Good book are a way for God to show you and to direct you in everything that you do.

In some cases it very well may be a piece overpowering while choosing to concentrate on your Bible. There is a ton of data, and you could have no clue about where to start. On the off chance that you are not excessively certain where to begin, there are such countless astounding assets. You can find dedications books, understanding plans, and Bible studies on the web or at your neighborhood book shop, and begin setting aside a few minutes for God He generally knows what is best for yourself as well as for your life. Since He will constantly set aside a few minutes for you, you really need to set out time for God day-by-day until it becomes a habit.

PRAYER POINT: *Lord please help me draw near to you and let me be lost in you, in Jesus name we pray, AMEN.*

DAY TWENTY
TOPIC: TALK TO GOD EVERYWHERE

Bible Reading: Proverbs 15:3

3 "The eyes of the Lord are in every place; Keeping watch on the evil and the good".

Memory Verse: Numbers 14:21

21 "but truly, as I live, all the earth shall be filled with the glory of the Lord".

Massage

I realize this one could appear to be somewhat unusual. How might you converse with God everywhere, or as the scripture says, "pray continually?" (Ephesians 6:18). Essentially, this implies that you ought to continuously have an outlook of petition and God ought to continuously be first in your heart even over the course of the day. Thus, when you have an extreme errand to finish at work, your most memorable idea is to ask God for help. Or on the other hand, when something extraordinary occurs for you, the primary thing you do is say thanks to God.

God is an "individual God," implying that he isn't far away and possibly answers when you have an otherworldly need. As a matter of fact, God is with us constantly and he needs to hear from us pretty much, all things, the good, the bad, the ugly, the big, and the small. You just only need to communicate with Him anywhere you find yourself. Let Him be your companion and friend at all time.

PRAYER POINT: *Oh Lord, let your glory fill all the earth, in Jesus name we pray, AMEN.*

DAY TWENTY ONE

TOPIC: LISTEN TO GOD'S VOICE AND PRACTICE OBEDIENCE TO HIS WORD

Bible Reading: Proverbs 4:20-23

20 "My son, give attention to my words; Incline your ear to my sayings.
21 Do not let them depart from your eyes; Keep them in the midst of your heart;
22 For they are life to those who find them, And health to all their flesh.
23 Keep your heart with all diligence, For out of it spring the issues of life".

Memory Verse: Psalm 119:105

105 "Your word is a lamp to my feet; And a light to my path.".

Massage

A relationship is a two-way road, correct? In this way, while conversing with God is significant, paying attention to Him is similarly as essential. Truly, God is continuously talking however now and then we neglect to hear him. We can get diverted by such countless things including virtual entertainment, television, our companions, and even work. Be certain that you're not allowing any interruptions to impede you hearing God's voice. I can go into more on hearing God's voice however I'll save that for another article.

It's adequately not to simply tune in; we ought to act in dutifulness when He talks. I realize dutifulness seems like such an unforgiving word. In any case, the bible really says that the people who love God will submit to his words (John 14:15). Submitting to God has a ton to do with confiding in him. At the point when we have little to no faith in him, we will generally do something contrary to what he says to do. At the point when we have little to no faith in him, it's likewise generally in light of the fact that we haven't yet fostered a profound relationship with him. The scripture says that if you hearken diligently unto his word, you will eat the good of the land (Isaiah 1:19). So, as believers, obedience unto God is not something to be debated about, it is sorely our access code into Gods supernatural blessings.

PRAYER POINT: *Oh Lord, help me to experience your light upon all my ways, in Jesus name we pray, AMEN.*

DAY TWENTY-TWO

TOPIC: INVITE HIM TO COME CLOSE

Bible Reading: 1 John 5:14-15

14. Now this is the confidence that we have in Him, that if we ask anything according to His will, He hears us.
15. And if we know that He hears us, whatever we ask, we know that we have the petitions that we have asked of Him".

Memory Verse: Romans 8:28

28 "And we know that all things work together for good to those who love God, to those who are the called according to His purpose".

Massage

Jesus makes reference that nobody comes to the father besides through Him. Jesus is the way and the main way. God calls us to have faith in Jesus. He wants us to recognize that Jesus is His child and that He passed on for us all so we might be saved. He additionally believes us should assert that Jesus miraculously came back to life and is presently situated at His right hand. Not one individual can deny Jesus and guarantee that they know God.

God needs a good nature, so that is the thing you need to give Him. To acknowledge Jesus, you should put stock in your heart that He really is the Child of God. You should likewise concede that you are a delinquent and with God's assistance, you will get some distance from every single sin. So how can you grant Jesus access to your heart? While kneeling down with your eyes shut and arms open wide, verbally welcome Jesus into your heart. Ask and say thanks to Him for pardoning. Likewise, share with Him that you accept that He died for you. Let him know that you are prepared to make Him Lord over your life. Basically converse with Him and let Him in on the admissions of your heart. Doing this with an earnest heart, unquestionably, will attract you nearer to God.

PRAYER POINT: *Oh Lord, please incline your ear to our prayer as we pray to thee, AMEN.*

DAY TWENTY-THREE

TOPIC: TAKE THE TIME TO TOUCH BASES WITH GOD

Bible Reading: John 14:16-17

16. And I will pray the Father, and He will give you another Helper, that He may abide with you forever.
17. the Spirit of truth, whom the world cannot receive, because it neither sees Him nor knows Him; but you know Him, for He dwells with you and will be in you".

Memory Verse: Psalm 34:8

Oh, taste and see that the Lord is good; Blessed is the man who trusts in Him!

Massage

We ought to be ceaselessly looking for God. In any case, how frequently do we truly associate with Him? Is it consistently? Once a year on Christmas? Anything your response is, we need to assist you with interfacing with God. When you begin pursuing a more profound relationship with God, you should direct your child to do likewise! However, associating with God ought to impede all the other things. In this way, here are a few hints on how we can focus on our associations with God notwithstanding our mind-boggling plans.

Jesus didn't provide a general order to "seek God personally." He didn't hoist individual closeness with God regardless of anything else. His words explicitly advise us to pursue "the realm" and "His exemplary nature." Those two equal direct objects of the action word "look for" are where we ought to center. God had been intending to lay out his realm and his honesty on earth for quite a while. Furthermore, he had an unmistakable vision for what those things would resemble. Therefore, take your time to seek Him first, prioritize your pursuit for Him and every other things shall be attached to your life (Matthew 7:7).

PRAYER POINT: ***Lord please help us to trust in you always, AMEN.***

DAY TWENTY-FOUR

TOPIC: OBEY GOD'S COMMANDMENTS.

Bible Reading: John 14: 14-15

14. You are My friends if you do whatever I command you.
15. No longer do I call you servants, for a servant does not know what his master is doing; but I have called you friends, for all things that I heard from My Father I have made known to you".

Memory Verse: John 15:9

As the Father loved Me, I also have loved you; abide in My love.

Massage

On the off chance that you comply with God's orders, you have faith in Jesus Christ, that He is God's Child, and you love each other. We give up all we are and all we need to Jesus Christ and to adoring each other. Except if we are doing these two things, we don't know God. Come what may an individual might say, he doesn't know God in the event that he has never given his life to Jesus Christ.

Furthermore, he doesn't know God assuming he scrutinizes, protests, and slanders his sibling and commits infidelity, kills, takes, lies, wants, or does anything more against his sibling. On the off chance that an individual truly knows God, he needs to satisfy God. He needs to discover increasingly more about God, and the main way he can discover increasingly more about God is to follow God. He needs to do the things that God does, to walk and cherish as God strolls and loves. The more we walk and love as God does, the more we will come to know God.

Certain individuals need to know God so they start searching for God. They search for God however they do it in incorrectly. Jesus said in His word that only those that seek Him diligently will find Him.

PRAYER POINT: *Help us to know you in all our endeavors, in Jesus name we pray, AMEN.*

DAY TWENTY-FIVE

TOPIC: CONTINUE WORKING ON YOUR SALVATION.

Bible Reading: Philippians 2:12-13

   12, Therefore, my beloved, as you have always obeyed, not as in my presence only, but now much more in my absence, work out your own salvation with fear and trembling;

   13. for it is God who works in you both to will and to do for His good pleasure".

Memory Verse: Philippians 4:1

Therefore, my beloved and longed-for brethren, my joy and crown, so stand fast in the Lord, beloved".

Massage

Working our salvation is altogether different from working for our salvation. At the point when Paul tells believers they need to sort out their salvation, he is basically making sense of that the magnificent present they uninhibitedly got from God is within them. We draw out those lovely ascribes and character attributes with conviction. Faith is a rest, yet faith works, not us. So working out what is within us is leaning on an unshakable faith.

This process can be startling initially as another believer finds how to live and walk by faith. Some solid fear might be available at first when an individual chooses to trust God as their source and harmony. I recall how frightening it was for me to quit confiding in my inherent capacities and have confidence in God's word. This is the very thing that Paul is alluding to when he specifies "fear and trembling". He isn't talking of fearing God. Rather, he is assisting the new believers with realizing that at the outset, it will appear to be startling to live by faith. Nonetheless, it is the best way to see our inward salvation manifest outwardly through our personality.

PRAYER POINT: *Help us to so stand fast in you Lord, AMEN.*

DAY TWENTY-SIX

TOPIC: DON'T COMPARE YOUR RELATIONSHIP WITH GOD TO THAT OF OTHERS

Bible Reading: 2 Corinthians 10:12

> 12. For we dare not class ourselves or compare ourselves with those who commend themselves. But they, measuring themselves by themselves, and comparing themselves among themselves, are not wise".

Memory Verse: Philippians 2:3
Let nothing be done through selfish ambition or conceit, but in lowliness of mind let each esteem others better than himself".

Massage

There's an enormous issue of comparison inside our present reality. I get it most likely has to do with web-based entertainment and our steady admittance to one another's features of life. Be that as it may, if you need to have serious areas of strength for a relationship with God, you need to defeat comparison. The grass isn't generally greener on the opposite side and the following young lady's relationship with God won't look anything like yours.

I remember back in school, I got together with a gathering of companions for supplication. Some of them were supplicating clearly, strong petitions as they walked forward and backward on the floor. Some others supplicated persuasive petitions and I asked why I was unable to get my words together like theirs. In any case, God simply wanted me to pray like me. He needed to hear my voice, not my best impersonation of another person. Very much like supplication, our relationship with God isn't a rivalry. It's not something worth talking about to be looked at. It's a sacrosanct sort of partnership among God and ourselves.

PRAYER POINT: ***Lord please Help us never to our infirmities and may we find solace in your word, AMEN.***

DAY TWENTY-SEVEN
TOPIC: PLACE YOUR REQUEST BEFORE GOD
Bible Reading: Hebrews 4:16

16 "Let us therefore come boldly to the throne of grace, that we may obtain mercy and find grace to help in time of need".

Memory Verse: Jonah 2:7
When my soul fainted within me, I remembered the Lord;
And my prayer went up to You, Into Your holy temple".

Massage

So let me ask you this: When you pray, do you implore general, clearing supplications for endowments, or have you taken in the mystery of getting explicit with God when you ask? That sort of unclear, general petitioning God might be charming for a small child, however as you fill in your daily life with the Almighty, He anticipates that you should get strong, fearless, and unmistakable about the things you request of Him.

So let me urge you today to open your bible and investigate its pages until you find explicitly what the desire of God is for your circumstance. When you know it, be guaranteed that you have the right as a child of God to go straight into His presence and, with honor and regard, demand that His will be done in this! As a matter of fact, God believes you should come to Him strongly like that!

In the event that you have a particular request, you should be explicit when you get some information about His will regarding this situation you're bringing before Him. You'll possibly encounter perceptible solutions to supplication assuming you get explicit when you implore. So make this the day you conclude you are moving forward higher in your time spend in meditation!

PRAYER POINT: ***Help us to ask rightly, may we never pray amiss, in Jesus name we pray, AMEN.***

DAY TWENTY-EIGHT
TOPIC: SEEK HELP FROM GOD

Bible Reading: Mark 10:27

> 27. But Jesus looked at them and said, "With men it is impossible, but not with God; for with God all things are possible."

Memory Verse: Psalm 105:4
Seek the Lord and His strength; Seek His face evermore!

Massage

Good morning, we are sometimes afraid or anxious about some circumstance or situation that we are going through and from a humanity stand point it can be seen as understandable. Though actually when we choose to step out on faith and trust God in all of our ways we should look to Him as the source of everything, for direction and comfort. Many times, we try to handle situation without Your consultation and can actually find ourselves digging deeper into problems rather than finding a solution. Only God can help us.

Seeking the Lord implies seeking for his presence. "Presence" is a typical interpretation of the Hebrew word "face." In a real sense, we are to seek for his "face." Yet this is the Hebraic approach to approaching God. To be before his face is to be in his presence.
Yet, aren't his children generally in his presence? Indeed and negative. God is omnipresent and in this manner generally close to everything and everybody. He holds everything in being. His power is ever-present in maintaining and administering all things. Therefore, whatever sort of help you desire in life, simply call upon His, and He will come to your aid. (Jeremiah 33:3).

PRAYER POINT: *Help us to experience the possibilities that only you can offer, in Jesus name we pray, AMEN.*

DAY TWENTY-NINE

TOPIC: YOU CAN DO ALL THINGS THROUGH HIM

Bible Reading: John 15:1-4

1. I am the true vine, and My Father is the vinedresser.
2. Every branch in Me that does not bear fruit He takes away; and every branch that bears fruit He prunes, that it may bear more fruit.
3. You are already clean because of the word which I have spoken to you.
4. Abide in Me, and I in you. As the branch cannot bear fruit of itself, unless it abides in the vine, neither can you, unless you abide in Me.

Memory Verse: Philippians 4:13
I can do all things through Christ who strengthens me".

Massage

Life is for the living and not every day will be lived as we hope that it will be, as trouble if not in our face, is just around the corner. That is why we should show wisdom as well as discretion so that we are operating on our solid foundation of faith. We can do nothing good in and of ourselves, only through Jesus Christ, we can do anything.

We all have experienced ups and downs while in the land of the living, that is the reward of being alive. On the other hand we can experience no more tears, sorrow or pain, though we cannot live. We have to make up our mind which do we really want to do. Do we want to live or do we want to die? One thing is for certain we cannot do both. Choose Jesus Christ and live. Though the reward of how we choose to live will certainly be rewarded accordingly, after awhile. With Jesus alone, we can do all things because He is the ultimate source of our strength. (Philippians 4:13).

PRAYER POINT *Provide Your peace to cover Your people to provide Your calm as we pray in Jesus name, AMEN.*

DAY THIRTY
TOPIC: YOU WILL OVERCOME

Bible Reading: Isaiah 43:1-2

1. But now, thus says the Lord, who created you, O Jacob, And He who formed you, O Israel. Fear not, for I have redeemed you; I have called you by your name; You are Mine.
2. When you pass through the waters, I will be with you; And through the rivers, they shall not overflow you. When you walk through the fire, you shall not be burned, Nor shall the flame scorch you.

Memory Verse: Psalm 46:1
God is our refuge and strength, A very present help in trouble".

Massage

We tend to allow what is going on around us to become us. The problems that we are totally committed to at most times is not ours to resolve. When we choose to take on extra stressful weight it can indeed become burdensome. The good news is that we have a Father who requests that we bring these burdens to Him and He will give us rest, (Matthew 11:28-30). God wants us to be focused more on Kingdom Building rather than playing in the sand where we can lose our footing and is not a good place to build a foundation.

Frankly, despite the fact that the greater part of us seem, by all accounts, to be alright and say that we are accomplishing something useful - a large number of us are going through times of substantialness, preliminaries, disappointments, forlornness, vulnerabilities and infections. Be that as it may, I need to remind you dear family of a Deliverer who looks after you and me when our boat rocks through a tempest.

PRAYER POINT *Lord we are grateful for this day, for Your grace, mercy and faithfulness towards us. Help us to bring our burdens to You as Your shoulders are well able to handle the load and we will acknowledge You in all of our ways in Jesus name we pray, AMEN.*

Conclusion

A prominent Bible scholar once said: "Take from a man his wealth and you hinder him; take from him his faith and hope and you stop him." The Bible says that without faith it is impossible to please God. (Heb. 11:6.) In fact, without faith you cannot walk with God. If you cannot please God without faith, then please Him by your faith in Him and in His Word.

To believe that there is a Supreme Being Who created heaven and earth is one thing. To believe and place confidence in Him to rule and reign in your life is another issue. That is where your faith comes in. The answer to facing the trials and tribulations of life lies in trusting God to bring you through them to life's highest point. Faith is the active force which draws the thin line between success and failure. Faith in God through Christ declares, "The Lord will bring me to a successful end." (Josh. 1:8; Jer. 29:11.)

A great man once said, "What you have undeveloped in you has no value." This book will show you how I placed value on my faith, and by so doing was able to face and triumph over the challenges in my life. Faith in God changed my destiny and that of millions of people with whom I have shared that faith around the world. I say to you, "Arise in your faith; use it in your challenges and difficulties time.

No force, demon, or power of darkness can stop a person who has faith in God through the all-conquering Jesus Christ. Whatever your situation or circumstance, set your eyes by faith on the Lord, keep looking to Him, and continue looking until the tide turns in your favor.

The Apostle Peter did not know or follow this principle at first, as he walked on the Sea of Galilee toward Jesus. (Matt. 14:22-31.) Fickle mindedness and wavering faith were the cause of his undoing. In your faith walk you must watch out for these things too. Stay calm and trust in the power of God's might.

Remember, ...the battle is not yours, but God's (2 Chron. 20:15). We Christians are the apple of God's eye, and anything that touches us touches Him. (Zech.2:8.) As children of God, redeemed though the finished work of Jesus Christ on the cross of Calvary, we are saved by faith (Eph. 2:8,9) and afterwards live by faith. (Rom. 1:17; Gal. 2:20.) Many of those Christians who have failed did so because they refused to follow the Biblical standard of walking day by day with Christ, their Savior and Lord, in trusting faith. God's intention is that we continue triumphantly through every circumstance and situation of life.

But is it possible to accept Christ and receive salvation by faith, only to turn around and live through the arm of flesh? Beloved, it does not work: This I say then, Walk in the Spirit.... For we through the Spirit wait for the hope of righteousness by faith. Galatians 5:16,5

It is clear from the above verses that looking for the hope of righteousness in Christ requires nothing less than walking in the Spirit through constant faith in Christ. To receive and appropriate the promise of power for your zero hour, you must understand the role of faith in the Christian walk.

The Gospel of John establishes that faith comprises one-half of a formula: the other half, which must always be included, takes the form of action. When Jesus speaks of faith, He refers to it as being revealed in action. This truth is illustrated by the lowering of the man "sick of the palsy" through the roof by his faithful friends (Mark 2:4), and the touching of the hem of Jesus' garment by the woman with the issue of blood (Matt. 9:20-22), Beloved, as a Christian, a sound understanding of faith will make a world of difference in your life. I have placed in your hands the secret to happy, abundant, and successful life. This secret worked for me. God can make it work for you too. Have faith in God!